THE KEY TO A SUCCESSFUL MARRIAGE

A How-to Manual for a Happy Marriage

by

Annie D. Maggard

Content

Introduction

Weddings are a lot of fun, but being married isn't always a piece of cake, despite all the dancing and laughter. (At other times, it resembles the piece of icing that got stuck in your nose during the smash—good intentions, bad result.) Whether you've been married for a long time or recently got hitched, living "happily ever after" requires a lot of work.

Chapter 1

To start, even happy couples have disagreements.

No marriage experiences constant happiness. There are ups and downs in relationships. When couples do argue, happy marriages listen to each other's viewpoints, spot when the conversation is losing steam, and fix the problem. The fact is that some of the happiest couples Dr. Juliana Morris have worked with "have withstood bad times," according to the family and couple therapist. Therefore, having occasional disagreements or going through a difficult time with your spouse does not necessarily indicate that your marriage

is miserable. In fact, it's likely a sign that you're normal.

Utilize each other's advantages.

It's not always easy to look past tiny irritations, and there may even be occasions when you resent your partner. But in order to have a good marriage, you must be able to set reasonable expectations and accept your partner's skills and weaknesses. For instance, if you are better at math, try not to get upset when they balance the checkbook incorrectly. Make it your responsibility to set the budget instead. If cooking is their specialty, they can handle dinner preparation instead. "Daily use of our strengths is related to better well-being," Additionally, we feel higher relational satisfaction when we

encourage our spouses to play to their strengths.

Don't look to your partner to make you whole.

The truth-check A fictional character named Jerry Maguire was beautiful when he said, "You complete me, but that's not how it works in the real world." It might result in an overly dependent relationship where neither of you is developing personally if you depend on your spouse to make you happy. She argues that in a successful relationship, partners should "complement," not "complete," one another. "We must be open to the other while remaining safe, mature, and complete in ourselves."So, rather than waiting for your partner to fill the hole,

be sure to foster your own interests and wants by enrolling in a class you're interested in or making arrangements with friends.

But continue to work together. Together, enjoy yourself.

To keep a good marriage, it's essential to not completely rely on your spouse, but it's also critical to share mutual experiences. "Attach new hobbies and profit to your relationship might make it stronger."

When a couple pursues a special interest or develops a talent together, such as taking tennis lessons or culinary classes, they grow closer. Happily married couples have a zest for life with one another, claims Morris. These experiences strengthen their relationship, whether it's through a

shared love of travel, a strong desire to start a family, or a commitment to a cause.

Decide to be drawn to your spouse.

Whether you find your partner attractive is up to you. You guessed it—yes. By practicing "attraction thoughts," you may decide if you're attracted to your spouse at any point in your marriage. Focus on the qualities you are most drawn to in your partners, such as their amazing legs or the way they raise your children (it need not be physical), she advises, in order to achieve this. The good news is that you can be attracted to someone even if they aren't a cover model. "Physical

attraction goes much beyond appearances."

Join in the laughter.

Since life is difficult, it's helpful to be able to find humor even when things are at their worst. Morris advises couples to laugh in both good and bad situations because "often when a couple has humor, it indicates they have perspective." She claims that happily married couples seem more at ease with one another. She thinks that sharing laughs with your spouse, whether it be through small inside jokes, an unexpectedly amusing text, or even just

binge-watching your favorite comedy, may strengthen your relationship.

Be considerate of one another.

Being respectful of and understanding of your spouse is crucial. Criticism and judgment frequently result in bitterness and defensive response. So, to maintain harmony in your marriage, refrain from criticizing your spouse's personality when you're angry. For instance, she advises against saying, "You're such a slob! Your dishwashing

is never done. Try something similar, "Because I made supper, I'd really love it if you could wash the dishes tonight," as an alternative. See how much more pleasant that sounds?

Celebrate the little victories.

Most of us know that it's important to be there for our partners during tough times, but couples frequently miss those chances to connect. It's equally important to acknowledge the good times since good things actually happen more frequently than bad ones. Therefore, she advises, "Immediately stop what you are doing and devote

your complete attention" the next time your husband mentions something wonderful, like a compliment from their boss. Asking inquiries and aggressively expressing joy at the excellent news would "help them savor the moment." By doing this, you'll express your appreciation for your marriage's joyful times.

Respect each other.

It's easy to take someone for granted when you're constantly around them, so thank them openly every day. We all need to be acknowledged and reinforced for the good things we do, whether it's praising them for something nice they did or telling them something you like about them. If your partner brings you coffee in the morning, for instance, tell

them it made your day. "If we failed to appreciated, we could get angry and distant from each other."

Accept change and prepare for it.

Couples must be willing to change and evolve in order to have a truly happy marriage. "Relationships thrive, people, expand, and our requirements switch constantly," Therefore, "What we need now might not be what we need in a few

years." "A balanced dance must bend. Because in a healthy marriage, one partner helps the other change into their best selves, which calls for both individual and collective maturation. up to the end of time.

Chapter 2:

This Counsel Might Preserve a Marriage

You could be concerned that your marriage is in trouble if your spouse has

changed from being your greatest friend to feeling like a complete stranger. However, deciding to obtain a divorce is a big step, especially if there's a chance you can make up for what was lost. If saving your marriage is really what you want, stop searching for "signs you're in a loveless relationship" and start attempting to rescue what's left of your relationship instead. Here is what we discovered:

Recognize what is effective.

It's likely that there are wonderful times in your relationship as well, but it can be challenging to find them when there is so much conflict. Every marriage experiences rough patches, but being able to see the good things is what helps people get through them. Changing

your inner conversation when you're not content with your relationship is one technique to do this. For instance, try expressing, "I'm pleased they have the weekends free to spend time with the family" instead of, "I'm so annoyed that they're never home for supper." By changing your perspective to be more optimistic, you can accept more and perhaps restore the friendship and trust that felt lost.

Observe the positive.

Did you adore traveling to new locations together when you first met? Did you both crack each other up? When a marriage is in trouble, it's critical for both parties to make an effort to recognize and recall the qualities that initially drew you to one another; if this

is possible, there may be "a glimmer of hope." Rebuild what is broken using those emotions and experiences as the basis.

Recognize the past.

Perhaps one of you had a liaison. Or maybe you learned something about your relationship that completely shocked you. Whatever it is, it's critical to accept what happened and dedicate yourself to a fresh start if you've both agreed to move forward together. This may entail mourning the loss of your relationship's former idealized state and accepting that it has evolved into

something else. Talk To Me Like I'm Someone You Love, author Nancy Dreyfus concurs. She says you don't want a band-aid solution. "Recreate something fresh, with greater transparency" is the better approach.

Be receptive.

Understanding your partner's perspective can be challenging, particularly when you disagree. However, Dreyfus argues that in order to save a marriage, "couples need to be able to listen to something that sounds completely ludicrous, and still see how it looks to their partner." Saying words like, "It's hard to accept, but I can see

why you would fantasize about other people," are a few examples of what this might include. Although it could be unsettling, "you are not betraying yourself." Instead, what you are doing is confirming your partner's reality and moving your relationship in the right direction.

Spend some time on yourself.

Do you rely on your partner to fulfill all of your needs? If so, marriage might have a serious impact. We can't rely on our partners to meet all of our needs. We "have the obligation to have dynamic lives with networking, friendships, and activities that ensure

we are living our best lives," she says, in order to have a successful marriage. Being comfortable in your own skin makes it easier to be comfortable in a partnership. We are all still developing.

Prioritize your relationship.

"The relationship needs to be improved on by both parties in the marriage," But to accomplish this, each person must be self-aware and role-reflective. urges you to consider whether you are making an effort in your relationship or whether you are simply leading parallel

lives. She asserts that some couples simply require a "tune-up" and suggests date evenings or spending an uninterrupted weekend away to help rekindle the lost connection.

Recognize the things you can't change.

Every couple has its own unique set of issues that can never be settled. "These disagreements come back again and

again in a relationship." Instead of trying to win the fight every time these intractable problems do, couples should come to an understanding regarding the deeper significance of each other's perspective.

Never give up too quickly.

According to MacGregor, there may be some reluctance, which is understandable, but there needs to be a commitment to try to resolve the challenging issues. Each marriage and scenario is unique, so this process could take months or even years. The truth is that everyone has their own quirks, irritations, and particular issues. It's good for the marriage's success, she argues if each spouse understands that

they will fight no matter who they marry.

Request assistance.

You can read all the books and follow all the advice, but sometimes going to a licensed professional who can work with you and your spouse to solve certain concerns is the most successful course of action. According to her, a good marriage therapist should maintain as much objectivity as possible while encouraging and challenging both parties. "A marriage therapist can act as a coach, mediator, and teacher," Kitley advises contacting friends for suggestions to find a therapist that both of you feel comfortable with. Alternately, begin your search on Psychology Today, Zocdoc, or

GoodTherapy. As an alternative, if you belong to a religious group, inquire as to whether any of their clergy members have had counseling training.

Chapter 3

Tips on How to Develop Your Romantic Relationships

No matter how long you've been dating your partner—a few months or several decades—sex is undoubtedly a crucial aspect of a romantic relationship for

many people. However, sex is also an intensely private interaction that can be accompanied by a lifetime of traumatic events, insecurities, and anxieties, making it challenging to fully unwind and savor each passionate moment with another person. You might be silently doubting whether or not your spouse is content or even enjoying your time together if you're self-conscious about your sexual performance. It's very simple—and completely normal—to become preoccupied with your own thoughts when having sex, both in and out of the bedroom. We all have a history and deeply set notions about how the experience "should" go or how things "should" feel, and having sex with someone puts you in a vulnerable position.

You could be concerned that in order for your spouse to enjoy themselves, you'll need to do acrobatic feats of Olympic caliber or engage in exhaustingly long bedroom sessions. We enquired about the specifics of how to truly have excellent sex and be a better lover from a clinical psychologist and certified sex therapist Kelifern Pomeranz, PsyD, CST, of California. dread and judgment.

Connecting with yourself comes first, of course.

"You need to connect with yourself before you can connect with a partner in a meaningful way." It's understandable if you haven't felt comfortable enough to explore what you

enjoy sexually before partnering up with a partner because so many of us were raised to view masturbation and sexual pleasure as something shameful. If you are serious about developing into a better lover, one thing you should do on a consistent basis is engage in some form of self-love or self-pleasure exercise.

Start small if it seems overwhelming. A fantastic place to start is by just rewarding yourself with a romantic bubble bath or self-massage. Discovering what makes you happy, investigating your turn-ons and turn-offs, accepting your body, and learning how to say "no," "not now," and "yes" are all important."What you do not understand yourself, you cannot explain

to a spouse." She suggests engaging in mindfulness exercises, using sex toys, reading or listening to erotica, viewing educational films, and seeing a sex therapist.

Focus on improving your partner's communication.

Many people find it challenging to have open and honest conversations about sex in their relationships. Maybe you've tried before, but the conversation didn't go well. Or you worry that you'll say something inappropriate and upset

your partner's feelings. Or, even worse, you think your spouse should intuitively know what you want when you're in bed and you shouldn't have to explicitly state your preferences. " She claims, "To practice talking about more difficult topics, you may start by engaging in conversation on mildly frightful non-sex topics." You can start advancing in the sex world as your communication abilities improve. Playing a communication game in which you initially tell your partner what they do that makes you feel attracted to them could be entertaining. Consider engaging with a sex therapist if the discussion of sex is still problematic. "

Make time for sex; this is serious.

Scheduling sex isn't a bad idea, even if you feel like your entire life is planned out on a Google calendar. "We all know how challenging it can be given our busy lives, but there is still a fallacy that sex should be spontaneous." A planned "noon shag" during the workday might be extremely enjoyable. Sexy texts sent throughout the day might act as a steady buildup to a scheduled evening rendezvous. "

Along the way, communicate with your buddy.

Any sexual experience must start with enthusiastic consent, and there are several ways to make sure you both are. Instead of assuming that your partner

can read your mind, each person in the relationship needs to take responsibility for their own happiness and effectively communicate their wants and requirements. wants, and desires to one another." Do you like this or that? or nonverbally (by grabbing your partner's hand and moving it to a different part of your body).

In and out of the bedroom, show your mate how much you value them.

Pomeranz is a huge supporter of making time each day to express your gratitude. " Make sure your compliments aren't just about what your partner does—for example, "I appreciate that you picked the kids up after their playdate," but also about who they are, such as "I appreciate your warmth and compassion." Of course, sexy sentiments are also acceptable.

Couples might try a different version of this activity by sticking a blank calendar to their refrigerator and writing daily compliments to one another on it. This can foster more intimacy and connection and is a nice method to measure gratitude through time.

"Some partners want novelty, while others crave familiarity," Be open to

trying new things, but before you do, talk to your partner to make sure you're on the same page. Included are several approaches to this, including: "discussing your sexual inclinations, taking sexual aptitude tests online, and traveling to a sex shop and perusing the selections there." "If a partner expresses a desire for a more expansive sexual framework, honor the guts it took for them to discuss this with you and have an open mind even if it makes you uncomfortable at first,"

Accept awkwardness, even when something goes wrong.

Everyone has unintentional errors while having sex, and there will inevitably be times when things go awry. "Intimacy and sex don't have to be serious business," "Playfulness, laughing, and silliness may all play a significant role in creating an intimate connection. I frequently advise couples who struggle with perfectionism in the bedroom to embrace it by making an effort to be as awkward as they can. This might be a pleasant reminder that having sex should be enjoyable. "

Try to be present-focused.

Even if you sincerely love and value your companion, it's normal to occasionally wander outside of the present. We are only mortal! " Bring yourself back to the present moment through your senses when your mind wanders (for example, worrying about your body, wondering if your partner is having fun, or thinking about work or chores). Notice how your partner smells and tastes; concentrate on the texture and temperature of their skin; pay attention to the sounds that come from both of you, and play with the energy between the two of you. The thing that strengthens the connection with a spouse is being in the moment together. "

Remove the emphasis from a final outcome, such as orgasm.

There are a lot of reasons why you or your partner could not experience an orgasm, despite the fact that we're taught to think that sex is only pleasurable when both people do, and it's entirely okay. Goal-oriented sex "diminishes pleasure, joy, and true connection by removing us from the present moment." Sometimes this happens because one (or both) partners have performance anxiety or believe that orgasm is what they want, according to research.

Taking orgasm off the table and engaging in erotic play—slowly moving toward and away from feeling and pleasure—can be entertaining."Imagine that you and your partner are dating

and that this is your first time examining each other's bodies." Without the strain of sex, it can still be a lot of fun to engage in activities like reciprocal masturbation, couples massage, or simple couch cuddles.

When it's over, ask your spouse what they require.

You may both learn to enjoy each other after sex by making small gestures like getting your spouse a snack and a drink of water, or even a warm blanket so they can go to sleep. Since your partner's post-sex desires may differ from your own, having a conversation about what they want and need can be helpful. Communication is key. Read: Your partner might want to snooze

alone, whilst you might prefer to cuddle up next to someone. All options are acceptable.

Chapter 4

Five Ways to Increase Emotional Intimacy in Any Relationship.

chuckle with a friend who shares your enjoyment of horrible puns. When the doctor calls you back regarding your test results, your lover squeezes your hand. a batch of cookies that your neighbor dropped off for no reason. Although they may seem insignificant in

the larger scheme of things, these moments are what create emotional intimacy—that sense of comfort and security you experience in intimate relationships. He likens the development of romantic and platonic relationships to that of water and sunlight. In addition to fostering the partnership's growth and fortifying the emotional link so that it can endure the winds of change, stress, and time apart, she says that this action "helps deepen the roots of the relationship by basing it on mutual trust and understanding."

Each partnership will experience intimacy differently, of course. Emotional intimacy can take many different forms depending on who it's with, just like physical closeness can range from high-fives or hugs to kissing or sex. It's important that you both feel

secure enough, to be honest, and open with one another. In other words, you can be who you truly are. There are numerous ways to accomplish this. But every method for fostering emotional closeness shares one crucial element: "Developing emotional intimacy in any relationship necessitates setting aside time to purposefully connect."

Here are five strategies for doing that.

They have set hours for check-in.

Sure, it technically counts as communication when you discuss who will handle the shopping and supper with your partner every day or when

you like all of your best friend's vacation photos on social media. But it's not the kind of honest conversation that deepens your emotional connection.

Set aside some uninterrupted time with your partner each week—say, 8:00 PM on Sundays—to sit and discuss your feelings. Fedrick advises that you "come prepared with what each of you wants to talk about." 'How did I meet your love language this week?' You might ask your partner something like, "What do you need from me this week?" or "What other questions do you have for me?"

Making time for your close pals on a daily basis can help you get into a similar routine. If they live nearby, schedule a regular monthly coffee or lunch date. For those who live far away,

schedule regular times for calls via FaceTime.

Accept your comfort zone.

Sharing a little more personal information is one of the easiest ways to advance any kind of relationship. It should feel suitable for the connection and be in your "stretch zone," which means it should seem a little more vulnerable than what you'd ordinarily share but not so vulnerable that it overwhelms you.

This might take the form of discussing some of your interests or being honest about a little issue you're trying to resolve in new connections. You may start by mentioning a program you're watching or a delicious recipe you've attempted to a neighbor or acquaintance. It's low-risk, but this information says something about you. Or talk to another mom at soccer practice about your daily struggle to convince your child to try more vegetables at dinner.

If after sharing, you feel a little more connected to the other person, you hit the mark. According to Stern, the contact should leave the other party feeling seen and included.

Say "thank you" or "well done."

Tell your closest friends and family members what you appreciate about them.

For every complaint or pushback, try to offer five compliments or praise. It can be easy to forget to express gratitude for all the little things, especially with romantic partners and to only speak up when something goes wrong. For example, clearing the table after breakfast or folding the laundry the way you like. Saying "Thank you for putting out the garbage" and "Thank you for working so hard for our family" repeatedly throughout the day is necessary.

Make plans for group activities.

Plan a date to do something you both like doing or something you need the other person's help with. Invite the person in your painting class to see a new exhibit at the nearby art gallery if they seem like potential friend material. Do you have a neighbor that wants to get in better condition with you? On Saturday mornings, we get together for jogs through the park. Self-disclosure frequently occurs spontaneously and is perceived as easier when you're involved in an activity that offers a small amount of distraction.

For the other person, be there.

A two-way street exists in emotional closeness. In order to show that you are there for a spouse, friend, or family member when they discuss anything sensitive or challenging with you, be compassionate or supportive in your response.

"Simply be present and listen" is one of the finest methods to accomplish it. After that, you can either ask them if they'd want to tell you more or affirm their feelings by saying something like, "I can understand why you'd feel that way." If it feels right, she advises, you can either ask how you can help or share a little piece of your own experience to let them know they're not alone.

And if you simply don't know what to say, Thank someone for sharing with you. It's always the right thing to do.

Simply expressing thanks can go a long way toward fostering a close emotional connection.

Chapter 5

Ten Keys To A Successful Marriage

Successfully married partners are astute. They research other successful marriages by reading books, going to seminars, reading online articles, and

more. Successful couples will, however, admit that they also pick things up via trial and error and through experience. I have worked with and observed hundreds of couples, and the following are 10 success principles I have discovered:

- **Happiness isn't the most crucial factor. Everyone wants to feel happy, yet it is a fleeting emotion. Successful couples discover how to deliberately take actions that will restore happiness when life takes it away.**

- **A successful married couple learns the importance of simply being there. Couples must persevere and support their partner when times are difficult and they are unsure of**

what to do. Couples often find a resolution over time when opportunities to relieve stress and conquer obstacles present themselves.

- **If you carry on, as usual, the outcome will be the same. Couples with common sense know that different approaches to challenges lead to varied outcomes. Frequently, small adjustments to one's strategy, outlook, and behavior have the largest impact on a marriage.**

- **Your attitude is important. Both changing behavior and attitudes are crucial. Bad attitudes can inspire negative emotions and behaviors.**

- **If you change your mind, your marriage will too. Couples' perceptions of one another are influenced by how they think and what they believe about their partner. It is crucial how they treat their spouse and what they expect from them.**

- **Where you water the grass, it grows the greenest. Successfully married couples have learned to reject the lie that "someone else will make me happy." They've learned to focus their efforts on improving their marriage and themselves.**

- **By altering yourself, you can change your marriage. Veteran couples have discovered that trying to change their partner is almost as difficult as pushing a rope. In our marriages, we frequently have no choice but to modify ourselves.**

- **Not merely a feeling, love is also a verb. The "feel-good side of marriage" erodes with time due to daily life. Happiness is one emotion that varies. However, true love is built on a couple's promise to be together "for better or for worse"—in good times and bad.**

- **Fighting the conflict between your ears is a frequent theme in marriage. Couples that have a happy marriage have learned to put their differences aside and refrain from bringing up the past. They themselves recall that both they and their spouse were flawed individuals when they were married.**

- **Marriage is not necessarily over after a catastrophe. Storms are like crises—loud, terrifying, and hazardous. But you must continue driving in order to get through a storm. A crisis might usher in a**

fresh start. Great people and successful marriages are born out of hardship.

Chapter 6

The Importance of Marriage

Many of the reasons why marriage is so important and the advantages it brings can be learnt and experienced by those who are already married. Or it's possible that some of you divorced because marriage wasn't for you and you found it too stressful. But there is still hope. But finding out that marriage can be more amazing than you have ever imagined or even experienced is where that hope begins.

I've been married a long time and have witnessed both fantastic and extremely

difficult things. My wife and I no longer feel lonely thanks to our marriage. Working as a team is more effective for us than working alone. We both have grown as a result of difficulties. As an added bonus, our relationship produced amazing children. All of those things are excellent and fantastic, but I've also learned something much better. I think God made marriage to show us more about who He is and how great He is. And numerous of his marital purposes make this clear.

Here are five reasons why marriage is so important.

- **Starting**

  In addition to forming a physical connection between two people, spiritual and emotional ties are also cemented in a marriage. Marriage marks the beginning of a new family and is a commitment that lasts a lifetime. In addition to this, it enables you to hone your selflessness as you look after your family, which includes your wife and your children. In addition to forming a physical connection between two people, spiritual and emotional ties are also cemented in a marriage. This marriage is a union, not unlike the one that exists between God and His Church.

- **Unity**

After getting married, a man and a woman are said to "merge into one." The tie that is created through marriage is one of a kind. Together, we are able to overcome the challenges of life, which in turn gives us with a life companion and a comrade.

- **Purity**

Purity is the goal of marriage. Almost every minute, temptation approaches us from all sides. Marriage provides us with the strength to resist temptation by fostering a strong, fulfilling love that both give to and receives from our spouse on a bodily, emotional, and spiritual level.

- **Parenting**

One of life's greatest blessings is having a kid naturally through marriage or through adoption. Approximately 40% of children growing up nowadays live without a father. That fact has astounding effects. Increases in mental and behavioral illnesses, criminal activity, and drug misuse are all brought on by fatherlessness. But when kids grow up in a happy marriage, they get to witness and experience the long-lasting advantages of a solid family firsthand.

- **Love**

  Marriage is intended to reflect the unwavering love of our Creator for us. It's a love that will always be there for us and won't ever abandon us. Contentment and joy come after a man and a woman have unconditional love for one another.

Chapter 7

Conclusion

You can have a happy and lasting relationship. In the midst of a hopeless marriage, there are steps you may do to heal and resurrect your relationship. Your marriage will be happier and more successful if you learn how to communicate, resolve disputes amicably, and avoid those that can't be solved. A happy marriage is based on how you handle disagreements and disagreements. Your marriage is in jeopardy if you use the four horsemen in your disagreements. The good news is

that the situation doesn't have to continue for long. You can save your marriage by fostering your feelings of love and adoration for your spouse. In addition, you should allow your spouse to influence you and convey the roles you desire to play in your marriage. You'll be able to enjoy a long-lasting marriage if you adopt and implement the key to a successful marriage.

www.ingramcontent.com/pod-product-compliance
Lightning Source LLC
LaVergne TN
LVHW050345160826
845677LV00014B/3790